FULL STUDENT GUIDE TO THE HARVARD REFERENCING STYLE

Easy Harvard Formatting Step by Step

CREATIVECLOUD PUBLICATIONS

Learn how to reference in the Harvard Style of Academic Referencing

There are several variations of Harvard style used in different countries. The following guide contains the most common format but is not the only one in use. If in doubt, consult your school's Harvard style guide.

The guidance is organized to provide you with the reference format for the main type of source material you may need to reference. Most sections also provide a range of examples on how your writing should be formatted:
1. The 1st part of this guide introduces Harvard referencing style and shows you the most common guidelines to format your academic paper.
2. The 2nd part of the guide shows you how to cite references in the main body of your essay.
3. The 3rd part of the guide shows you how to compile the reference list at the end of your essay.
4. The 4th part of the guide answers frequently asked questions.
5. The 5th part of the guide contains the paper layout example formatted in the Harvard Style.

This guide is intended to help you understand how to use source material effectively in this referencing style. It outlines the general features of the style, but it is important that you follow your department's specific guidelines as there are some different interpretations and requirements that might be specifically required within your discipline.

The instructor for your class is the final authority on how to format your References List.

CreativeCloud Publications 2020

PART 1: INTRODUCTION

General Approach

Referencing

Referencing is the process of acknowledging and recording details of the sources (books, journal articles, electronic sources etc.) you refer to in a piece of work. You need to accurately acknowledge these sources for several reasons:
- to demonstrate you have read widely about the subject you are writing about;
- to demonstrate how you have used the work of others to develop your own ideas;
- to support and evidence your arguments with appropriate academic theory, research and practitioner experience;
- to allow your tutor and other readers to easily check your sources to see which ideas and words are your own and which are from sources you have used as evidence to support your arguments and assertions;
- to give appropriate credit to the original authors;
- to protect yourself against any accusations of plagiarism.

Harvard Style

The Harvard style originated at Harvard University, but has been much adapted by individual institutions. There is no set manual or formatting rules for Harvard as there is for some other referencing systems.

Harvard is a style for citing sources by giving the name of the author and the date of their publication in the text of a piece of writing, within brackets ( ), for example (Smith, 2016).

A reference list of full bibliographic details is then given at the end, with sources listed in alphabetical order by author.

Areas of Usage

- Archaeology
- Biochemistry
- Biology
- Economics
- Environment
- Health Sciences
- Philosophy
- Politics
- Social Policy and Social Work
- Sociology
- Theatre, Film and Television
- Management

Why is Referencing Important?

Citing and referencing source material is a crucial aspect of academic writing. You will probably be aware that plagiarism (using someone else's work as though it were your own) is a serious form of academic misconduct and it must be avoided at all costs. Referencing accurately and consistently is an important part of ensuring the distinction is clear between your words and the words and ideas of others in your assignments.

The University regulations about plagiarism can be found in your Student Handbook.

Getting good marks for your assignment is dependent on many factors; one of them is accurately referencing the information sources that you have consulted. To get full marks for referencing, you need to follow the Harvard referencing style which is a widely accepted referencing system in higher education.

Referencing to existing theories, policy initiatives, research findings etc. is an essential part of academic writing and standard academic practice. It demonstrates the extent of your research and thereby reveals your understanding of the range and type of thinking in any given area.

In short, references are used to:
1. avoid plagiarism by acknowledging the source of an argument or idea help support your arguments;
2. show the full scope of your research.

Why Should I Reference?

If you fail to cite your sources, you can be accused of poor academic practice or even plagiarism. Therefore, you should reference:

- to demonstrate to your lecturer that you have conducted thorough research for your assignment;
- to provide your lecturer with the details of the sources that you have used so that they;
- follow up your research if they want to;
- to avoid facing academic penalties for plagiarism.

How Can I Avoid Plagiarism?

Referencing is an important skill for any student writing academic essays and projects. There is an expectation that your work will make use of existing sources. In order to avoid plagiarism, you must always acknowledge sources that you use that are not your own.

You may:
1. directly quote from a source;
2. paraphrase (writing another person's ideas in your own words);
3. summarize (pick out the key points of someone else's work).

You can avoid plagiarism:
- by appropriately acknowledging in your assignment text when you have referred to materials or ideas taken from other authors;
- by including a reference list at the back of your assignment with all the sources you have referred to in your work.

For all your sources you should make sure you know the answers to the following questions:

1. Who wrote the work?
2. When did they write it?
3. What is the name of the work?
4. Where can it be found?

You will find this information on the title page at the front of a book and it can also be found on the Online Library catalogue. If you do not have any part of the information, you will have to leave it out or indicate you do not have it. For example entering 'nd' if there is no date.

Do not just use as many references as you can in a bid to impress the marker that you've read a massive amount. Your references should be relevant.

When you submit your work it will be put through a plagiarism checker, which determines if there is any material that is incorrectly referenced.

How Do I Reference?

Students are required to acknowledge the sources they use in their written assignments. This process involves two steps:
1. Citing sources in your assignment text using in-text citations where you include usually the author, date and page number of the work.
2. The final list of references, which details all the sources you have cited from on a separate page at the end of the essay.

You can reference any sources using the Harvard system - the rule is to follow the basic order of information given below.
If you do not have any part of this information, you will have to leave it out and indicate that you do not have it.

Ideally, you should know who the author is, even if it is a corporate author rather than a specific person.

Harvard Referencing Style

General

Within your paragraphs, you should be sure to cite your sources using in-text citations and include them to references list at the end of the work.

In Harvard style, in-text citations use the author's name, the year of publication, and the page number on which the information appears:
- You should provide a citation for each fact, summary, paraphrase, or quotation you use from an outside source.
- An in-text citation to a quote from page 15 of a book by Donald Black would look like this (Black, 2018:15).

List your source at the end of the paper in the reference list. Such citations make it easy for readers to see where you gathered your information to check it for themselves.

Harvard style typically asks to use a standard font:
- Times New Roman, Arial, etc. at size 12 pt.
- You should not use fancy fonts, colors in the text, or excessive amounts of boldface, underlining, or italics.
- The whole paper should be double-spaced.

The rules for in-text mentions:
- The titles of books, movies, long plays, TV shows, journals, newspapers, magazines, and websites are Italicized.
- Short stories, poems, episodes of TV shows, and short plays are placed in "Quotation Marks."

Following these conventions makes it easy for readers to recognize what you are referring to quickly and accurately.

Cover Page

Harvard formatting requires a very specific title page:

- About halfway down the page is the title of the paper, in all capital letters.
- Following this (about three lines down) is the name of the author.
- Move four lines down and then put the name of the class.
- On the line after that, the name of the professor.
- Next line is the name of the school.
- Then the city and state where it is located.
- The date.

EXAMPLE:

THE HARVARD ESSAY TEMPLATE

by (Name)

The Name of the Class (Course)
Professor (Tutor)
The Name of the School (University)
The City and State where it is located
The Date

Header

The header contains a short description of the title and a sequential the page number:
- The title is right justified.
- There is only a partial title expressing the main idea in the essay.
- Between the partial title and the page number, there are exactly five spaces.

Using the example title "The American Storytelling" a partial title and page number in Harvard format could look like:

Storytelling   1

Headings

- If you have a long essay, use a new heading every time you change major topics:
    - Use centered headings to break up the body of the essay, uppercase.
- Subheadings may be used to introduce new subtopics:
    - Use italicized subheadings for subsections, uppercase, flesh left.

EXAMPLE:

Centered Headings Uppercase
Italicized Subheadings for Subsections

Body

Introduction

The first paragraph of the essay introduces the reader to your topic with a "hook," which might be an interesting fact, a statistic, or a lively quotation that sheds light on your essay.

Body Paragraphs

1. The first sentence of the first body paragraph should be the topic sentence, which tells the reader what the paragraph will discuss.
2. After the topic sentence, supporting details are used to provide more information about it. Details can include analysis, explanation, quotations about the subject, and/or facts and figures that support the topic sentence.
3. The paragraph should conclude with a sentence that sums up the paragraph and leads into the next body paragraph.

You should show how your next paragraph connects to the one that came before.

Helpful in linking paragraphs transition words:
- "similarly,"
- "however,"
- "therefore," etc.

As long as you are consistent, any UK date form is acceptable in text:
- 28th December 2019
- 28.12.2019
- 28.12.19, etc.

Conclusion

1. The first sentence of the conclusion should remind the reader in different words what the essay has shown.
2. You should then offer a brief discussion of your topic to remind the reader what the most important parts of the essay were.
3. You should finish your essay with the single most important point you want the reader to remember.

Figures

Figures are:
- Diagrams
- Pictures
- Photographs
- Tables
- Screen captures

Regardless of the creator of the figure you are referencing, you should cite the author or editor of the work in which you found it:
- The citation is as that for a direct quotation and the page number is included in the reference.
- Figures are usually accompanied by a brief description and are listed throughout a piece of work by figure number.

- If the item has been copied and amended by you, e.g. another axis added to a graph, then use amended from.
- If the item is your own original work, then use personal collection.
- You may also include the source medium in your citation.

EXAMPLES:

Figure 1. Strategies for ensuring high-quality tape recording (Poland, 2001:638)

Figure 2. Johannes Vermeer's The Girl with the Pearl Earring (Chevalier and Hale 2011:55)

Figure 3. Johannes Vermeer's The Girl with the Pearl Earring (amended from Chevalier and Hale 2011, p.55).

Figure 4. Coventry Cathedral (personal collection).

Figure 5. Plan of Activity (Makepeace, 2015, [screen capture])

- You should include a full reference to sources in the list at the end of your work.
- Your own original work should not appear in the list of references at the end, as it has not been published.

Abbreviations

ch. or chap. -> chapter
ed. -> edition
Ed. or Eds. -> editor(s)
et al. -> and others
n.d. -> no date
no. -> (issue) number
p. -> page (single)
pp. -> pages (page range)

ser. -> Series
supp. -> supplement
tab. -> Table
vol. -> Volume

Plagiarism and Copyright

Plagiarism

The misappropriation or use of others' ideas, intellectual property or work (written or otherwise), without acknowledgement or permission may include, but is not limited to:
- the importing of phrases from or all or part of another person's work without using quotation marks and identifying the source;
- without acknowledgement of the source, making extensive use of another person's work, either by summarizing or paraphrasing the work merely by changing a few words or by altering the order in which the material is presented;
- the use of the ideas of another person without acknowledgement of the source or the presentation of work which substantially comprises the ideas of another person and which represents these as being the ideas of the candidate.

Remember that you must acknowledge your source every time you refer to someone else's work. Failure to do so amounts to plagiarism, which is a serious offence.

For the avoidance of doubt, plagiarism may be intentional or unintentional.

Copyright

You do not have to seek permission to include third party copyright material in your academic work, as long as it is fully referenced.

PART 2: IN-TEXT CITATIONS

General

The Harvard system (Author Date Method):

All statements, opinions, conclusions etc. taken from another author's work (print, online or multimedia) should be cited, whether the work is directly quoted, paraphrased or summarized.

Referencing is a two-part process:
1. Citing in the text
2. References at the end of the work

The Harvard referencing system requires referencing in two places in your work. First, you must give a partial reference within your work, referred to as an in-text citation or reference, and secondly, you must give a full reference in a final list of references at the end of your essay.

An in-text citation may be included in several formats depending on how you have structured the sentence and whether you have quoted the text directly or not.

Page Numbering

You are required to include a page number at the point of citation when you have included a direct quotation. You may include a page number for a paraphrased quotation if you wish, but this is not compulsory. Many tutors argue that if you have paraphrased from a specific page, they would like to be able to find this page to ascertain if you have correctly interpreted the author's views.

The Harvard style requires you to include the name of the author and the date of their publication in ( ) and, when appropriate, to add a page number.

If you have included a direct quotation from an online source that has no page numbers you must write (Jackson, 2015, [online]); otherwise the marker may think you have omitted a page number.

Citations Structure

The Author's or Editor's Surname:

- If there are up to 2 authors you should include each author's surname.
- If there are more than 2 authors you only need to put in the first author's surname followed by 'et al'.
- If there is no named author you can use a corporate/organization author name (this is often the case for websites).
- If there is neither a named or corporate author you can use 'Anon' as the author's name.

The Year of Publication:

- You can find the publication date of a book in the first few pages.
- For a website, the publication date is usually at the top of the page.
- For a webpage, it may be preferable to cite the year in which the page was accessed, e.g. (ca. 2019), rather than use (no date).
- If an exact year or date is not known, an approximate date preceded by 'ca.' may be supplied e.g. (ca.1680).
- If you cannot find a publication date for a source put in

the initials "nd" which stands for 'no date'.

Pagination:

- When citing quotations from particular parts of a document, the location of that part (e.g. page number) should always be given after the year within the brackets.
- For e-readers, where pagination is absent, include chapter instead.
- For webpages and online newspapers, this detail is not required.
  - Each cited publication must have a corresponding full reference in the list of references at the end of your work.

Publication Titles

- When referring to a book, journal or newspaper in your text, always write these in italics.
- Make sure you capitalize the publication correctly.

EXAMPLES:

Naisby refers to *Every Child Matters* in her work on ...

In *The Sunday Times* (2014:12), Martins reports that ...

Integrating Quotations into the Work

The more sophisticated you become at incorporating quotations into your own prose, the more fluent and authoritative your writing will be. There are numerous phrase structures for introducing quotations:

EXAMPLES:

Fitzgerald identifies a link...
Strong and Overs found that...
Spinner et al. argue that...
Maxwell refutes Smart's claim...
Jackson supports this view...
Martin offers useful...
Green describes the impact of...
Cly's main argument that...
Peters suggests...
According to Miles...
Yates contends that...
As Davidson cites...
Awad comments that...
Freer et al. observed...
Merryman asserts...
Fontwell has shown...
Megginson (2009) provided an explanation for...

In this context, Black...
Jones claims that...
Mellers illustrates this by...
Vincent stated...
Homer et al. (2010) make a link...
Parry (2008) reasoned that...
Harvey values the...
Harrison confirms that...
Ever since Armon and Garing (2007) first showed...
... identified by Green and Grace as

Make sure you select the correct verb for the context:

Ensure you use the correct verb to introduce or explain your quotation. For example, one author may 'suggest' or 'imply', whereas another may 'infer' or 'deduce'. One author may be commenting or observing while another will be asserting or claiming.

Citing

- **Summarizing / Paraphrasing:**
  - Paraphrasing is rewriting an argument or restating information taken from someone else's work using your own words, phrasing and interpretation.
- **Quoting:**
  - Quoting is when you include the exact words from another author in your own writing. To accurately quote you need to enclose the word in quotation marks, and if it is from a book mention the page number the quote comes from.

When you summarize, paraphrase or quote a source, you must always cite the original author in your writing so that the reader is aware you are presenting or discussing another person's ideas and not your own.

The essential features of a citation are the author's last name, the year of publication and (when a direct quotation is used) the page number.

A colon should be used between the year of publication and the page number:
- (Smith, 2012:2)
- (Smith, 2012:15-16) *(when the quotation goes over two pages)*

When the citation comes at the end of the sentence the punctuation mark comes after the citation. It also comes after the quotation mark.

EXAMPLES:

As Grant (2006:74) explains 'the idea is that the coach primarily facilitates the construction of solutions rather than trying to understand the aetiology of the problem'.

According to Holbeche (2009), developing a strong employee brand is a key component to attracting prospective job candidates.

When using a direct quotation from an online source with no page number, include the word [online].

EXAMPLE:

Clement (2014, [online]) suggests 'literature might be made available to all relevant bodies'.

Summarizing

A summary is an extract of the main points from an original source, restated in your own words where possible, which presents the author's main idea or argument only.

It may be a summary of a passage of text or whole chapter or work. Since the summary may cover a number of pages, no page number is required.

Paraphrasing

Paraphrasing is expressing another person's ideas in your own words. It is more sophisticated than summarizing because it involves an element of interpretation, as you act as a mediator between the original author and the reader.

Paraphrasing can be used to demonstrate your own understanding and interpretation of what another author said, by expressing their ideas in your own words. You still need to include the author's name, year and page number in the citation, for an example "see Pears & Shields (2016:10-11)". The page number is not strictly required, but strongly recommended if you are paraphrasing from a specific quotation.

Try to paraphrase as much as possible in order to develop a fluid, critical style of writing. When paraphrasing, you must use your own words as far as possible. The purpose of paraphrasing is to enable you to more readily integrate sources' ideas into your critical writing.

Direct Quotations (Quoting)

Quotations are word-for-word text included in your work and must be clearly distinguished from your own words and ideas.

Quotations are the exact reproduction of the original author's words and should be used only when:
- the information presented by the original author is highly significant;
- paraphrasing the information would alter significantly the meaning of the original source;
- the purpose is to present the linguistic style of the original author.

Quoting Written Work

- Single or double quotation marks may be used but be consistent.
- Indented quotations need not include quotation marks.
- The page number needs to be included if it comes from a book, newspaper article etc. (not if it's taken from a website).

EXAMPLE:

'A written marketing plan is the backdrop against which operational decisions are taken' (McDonald & Wilson, 2011:30).

Quoting from Direct Speech

- Double quotation marks are used.
- No page number is mentioned.

EXAMPLE:

"One of the tests of leadership is the ability to recognize a problem before it becomes an emergency" (Glasgow, 1993).

- If you have quoted directly from or, paraphrased the source text, you need to include the page number.

GENERAL FORMAT:

(Author surname, year:page number)

EXAMPLE:

Bruner (1960:33) hypothesized that 'any subject can be taught to any child at any stage of...'

Short Quotations

Short quotations are direct quotations of fewer than two sentences:

- For short quotations (of up to 2 or 3 lines or of less than 40 words), use a brief phrase within your paragraph or sentence to introduce the quotation before including it inside double quotation marks " ".
- Direct quotations are sections of text which are copied directly from the source publication.
- If the quote is less than a line it may be included in the body of the text in double quotation marks ' '.

EXAMPLES:

It has been suggested that from the sociocultural perspective, learning is perceived as 'being embedded in social and cultural contexts, and best understood as a form of participation in those contexts' (Boreham and Morgan, 2008:72). There is a great deal of evidence to support this viewpoint ...

The research on staff-student collaboration 'explored

whether students could identify, enhance, evidence and evaluate their employability skills' (Dickerson et al. 2016:254).

As Neville (2010) emphasizes, "you should cite all sources and present full details of these in your list of references" (p.37).

Long Quotations

Long quotations are direct quotations of two sentences or more:
- For longer quotations (of 40 words or more) you use block quotation, clearly indented to indicate these words are not your own.
- Long quotations contribute to your word count and should be used sparingly.
- Long quotations do not have quotations marks. You may use a comma or colon at the end of the main body before starting the quotation if appropriate.
- Long quotations should be single-spaced.
- Long quotations need to be indented in its own paragraph by 1 cm, separate from the main body of your essay.
- Quotation marks are not used but you still need to include the author's surname, date and page number before or after the quote.

EXAMPLES:

With these dominant preferences in mind, Eseryl calls for a unifying model for evaluation theory:

> There is a need for a unifying model for evaluation theory, research and practice that will account for the collaborative nature of, and complexities involved in, the evaluation of training. None of the available models for training evaluation seem to account for these two aspects of evaluation. Existing models fall short in com-

prehensiveness and they fail to provide tools that guide organizations in their evaluation systems and procedures (Eseryl, 2002:96).

Dickerson et al highlight the complexity in characterizing students' roles within higher education:

> Whilst 'labelling' students as customer or consumer, for example, enables discussion of important issues in higher education it can conceal the complexity of engagements between participants, where individuals adopt multiple roles. Thus, a student might move fluidly between engaging as 'customer' when completing the UK National Student Survey, as collaborator or partner with academic staff and peers during a module session and as producer in another context.
>
> (Dickerson et al, 2016:260)

Neville (2010, p. 38) comments that:

> It can sometimes be difficult, if not impossible, to avoid using some of the author's original words, particularly those that describe or label phenomena. However, you need to avoid copying out what the author said, word for word. Choose words that you feel give a true impression of the author's original ideas or action.

Editing Quotations

Quotations should normally be reproduced exactly from the original source. If you modify a quotation, this must be acknowledged in one of the following ways:

Omitting Sections of a Quotation

- If you omit a part within a quotation, either for brevity or to ensure that it fits easily into your sentence structure, you must include three ellipsis points (...) to inform the reader.

EXAMPLE:

In the 1990s it was noticed that 'policy-makers turned to the school effectiveness and improvement tradition for support, largely because its explanations ... were consistent with their own assumptions' (Lauder et al., 2011:21).

Adding or Changing Words in a Quotation

- If you add or change words in a quotation to make its meaning clearer, these need to be identified by square brackets. In this example 'they' is replaced by [students].

EXAMPLE:

'Because the information [students] were exposed to was contextualised by objects, spaces, people and events, it made sense and could be remembered' (Hooper-Greenhill, 2007:154).

Highlighting Problems in a Quotation

- Original errors in a quotation (such as incorrect spellings/terminology) and misunderstandings or problematic details can be identified in your writing by inserting [sic] (Latin for 'thus' or 'so') at the appropriate point in the quotation.

EXAMPLE:

'In endeavouring to solve the simple question of the education of idiots [sic] we had found terms precise enough that it were only necessary to generalise them to obtain a formula applicable to universal education' (Montessori, 1917:81).

Citing in the Text

Citation Placement

- Place your citation where you feel it should naturally occur within a sentence.
- Depending on your writing style, it may follow a phrase/idea or appear at the beginning of a sentence or paragraph.

If the author's name occurs naturally in the sentence:

- If you have referred to the author's name in the main text, insert the publication year in brackets after the name:

GENERAL FORMAT:

> Author surname (Year)

EXAMPLES:

> Bruner (1960) suggests that...

> As Waring (2014:33) said, "theory and practice should not be seen as separate entities" and so...

> In his highly acclaimed study Waring (2014) argued that theory and practice should not be seen as separate entities...

If the name does not occur naturally in the sentence:

- After you have summarized an author's point, insert both the author's name and publication year in brackets.

GENERAL FORMAT:

> (Author surname, Year)

EXAMPLES:

It has been suggested that… (Bruner, 1960).

Theory arises out of practice and the two are therefore inextricably linked (Waring 2014).

Authors

- Use the name(s) of the person or organization shown most prominently in the source as being responsible for the published content.
- If no author is given and there is clearly no identifiable person or organization, use 'Anon.', except for webpages, newspapers, film, dictionaries or encyclopedias (see below).

Two Authors

- Texts that have two authors should be cited using both their surnames.
- Page numbers must also be included in the citation if quoting directly from the source.

EXAMPLES:

Researchers need to reconsider the use of digital video approaches and their potential to expand research imagination and support collaborative research (Gallagher and Kim, 2008).

Doole and Lowe (2012) proposed that…

Multiple Authors

- For texts that have multiple authors (more than two authors), it is necessary to mention the first author's surname followed by *"et al."* (an abbreviation of the Latin for 'and others') which is used in formal writing to avoid a long list of names and the year of publication.
- The *"et al."* may be in italics and followed by a full stop.
- Some earlier versions of Harvard guides require students to include all authors' surnames in full for the first citation, and thereafter use the *"et al"* convention.

EXAMPLES:

As global economies grow and the cost of doing business increases (D'Arienzo *et al.* 2016). A full list of all author's names should appear in the list of references at the end of your work.

Organisational Consultancy and executive coaching would appear, rather like in Dismith *et al.*'s (1997) study, to involve two different units of analysis.

No Authors

- Texts with no attributed author should be cited using the title and year of publication.
- When referencing the title of a book, publication, newspaper, film, play, etc., it should always be written in italics.

EXAMPLES:

The Oxford Atlas of the World (2013) illustrates …

This is illustrated in current representations of the marked geographical spaces (*The Oxford Atlas of the World*, 2013).

If no author is given and there is clearly no identifiable person responsible:

- For corporate author (organization), put name of publishing organization:

The Museum Association (2012) confirms that ….

- Where acronyms are commonly used for corporate/organizational authors, the first citation should be in full with the acronym in brackets after this. Subsequent citations may use the abbreviated form:

The Department for Education (DfE) (2013) states that…
… by the end of semester (DfE, 2013).

...by the end of semester DfE (2013).

- For webpages use the organization or company author:

In the *IPCC* (2016) report on Climate Change and Oceans and the Cryosphere...

- For newspaper articles use the newspaper title:

Social media is driving the rise of hate crime (*The Telegraph,* 2016).

- For a film, use the title of the film:

As typified by James Dean portraying the moral decay of American youth (*Rebel without a Cause*, 1955).

- For a dictionary or encyclopedia, the title of the work may be used:

According to the *Oxford Encyclopedia,* "A quotation from the text would be inserted here." (*Oxford,* 2007:375).

- For other sources, use 'Anon.':

In an earlier text (Anon. 1908) it was stated that...

No Date

- If no date is available, you can still use the quotation.

EXAMPLE:

'Non-existence is a concept that is meaningless by itself. It isn't something. It is a relational concept, gaining meaning only in comparison to another concept' *(TheImportanceofPhilosophy.com*, n.d.).

Multiple Citations for the Same Author

- If two or more references by the same author are cited

together, separate the dates with a comma.
- Start with the oldest publication.

EXAMPLE:

(Bryant, 2010, 2011, 2012).

Multiple Sources

If you are pulling together a number of sources (more than one source) to support your argument you may want to use a number of sources in one in-text citation:
- References to work from several sources require the surnames of each of the authors and the dates of each of the texts.
- It is usual to cite the texts in chronological order by date (earliest date first, then alphabetically by author surnames if two sources are published in the same year) or in order of academic relevance.
- If you are citing more than two sources, order by date and separate with a semicolon ";" within the same set of brackets.

EXAMPLES:

Jones (2009) and Wyness (2011) both argue that...

Shifts in the conceptual analysis of childhood reflect shifts in the social contexts for childhood (Jones, 2009 and Wyness, 2011).

As is widely stated in the literature... (Harris 2011; Hale 2012; Malcolm 2014)

The impact of environment and society on child development are demonstrated in the main learning theories (Piaget, 1954; Bruner, 1974; Vygotsky, 1978).

Authors with More than One Publication in a Year

- If citing from more than one work/document by the same author(s) published in the same year, it is necessary to add a suffix (lower case letters a, b, c etc.) after the year of each publication within the brackets.
- The letters should be assigned in chronological order of publication, if known.
- The letters after the date will determine the order in your list of references e.g. 'Fordham (2011a)' would be listed before 'Fordham (2011b)'.

EXAMPLES:

Fordham (2011a) discussed the subject...
...highlighted by Fordham (2011b).

In his research Smith (2015a) explores...
He also explains... (Smith 2015b).

Online Sources

- Citing from internet sources must follow the same principles as citing from hard copy, so the citation in your writing should identify the author and the date of publication, and include the page number if one is available.
- When citing a webpage on an organization or company website, use the organization or company as the author.
- Do not insert the URL (web address) in the body of your text.
- If you are using a direct quotation and you cannot trace a page number, you must include the word [online] in the citation.

EXAMPLES:

In Lithuania, governments were asked 'to undertake every reasonable effort to achieve the restitution of cultural assets looted during the war' (Payne, 2011, [online]).

Price Waterhouse suggest "A quotation from the relevant webpage would be inserted here." (Price Waterhouse 2011).

Scriptural Citations

- Bible, Koran/Qur'an, etc. should only be included in the text and not the list of references.
- Include book, chapter and verse. If quoting you may add the translation or edition.

EXAMPLE:

'He gives strength to the weary and increases the power of the weak.' (Isiah 40:29, New International Version).

Legislation

- UK Statutes (Acts of Parliament) should be cited in full.

EXAMPLE:

The Equality Act 2010 legislates that it is unlawful to discriminate on the grounds of...

PART 3: REFERENCES LIST

General

Check that you reference all sources used in two places:
1. in-text and
2. in your references list.

- If you include a citation (reference in-text) it must also appear in the list of references and vice versa.
- The full list of references should include only the sources you have explicitly referenced in the writing.
- Reference list should be presented on a new page at the end of your work.
- Always keep a record of your readings for your reference list while working on the paper.

Punctuation and Formatting

Harvard has no one true style of punctuation and it is not prescriptive about punctuation, so you will see variations between different publishers and researchers:

- The reference list comes at the end of your assignment and should be arranged in alphabetical order of author's surname.
- Each reference should start on a new line.
- If there is no author, the name of the website or corporate author, the title should be included in the alphabetical sequence.

- For printed material, where the exact date is unclear you could use 'circa' or 'c' before the date to indicate the approximate date of publication.
- Where an author has several texts included in the same reference list, these should be presented in chronological order if known. References to more than one work by the same author(s) published in the same year are differentiated by a letter suffix, which corresponds to the letter suffix used for the in-text citation, e.g. 2011a and 2011b.
- You should only capitalize the first letter of the first word of a book, journal article etc. The exception is the names of organizations.

The Basic Order of Referencing

GENERAL FORMAT:

> Author (Year) *Publication title.* Place of publication: Name of publisher.

EXAMPLE:

> Bruner, J.S. (1960) *The process of education.* Cambridge, MA: Harvard University Press.

Online Sources

If your source is available online rather than as a hard copy, you need to include one of the following types of link, depending on whether you have a URL or DOI.

URL (Uniform Resource Locator)

- This is the website address for the reference.
- Include: Available at: URL [Accessed: date] at the end of the reference, giving the day, month and year that you last accessed the website.

EXAMPLE:

> Available at: https://owl.purdue.edu/owl [Accessed: 29.12.19].

DOI (Digital Object Identifier)

- A DOI is a unique alpha-numeric identifier that locates individual digital (online) sources such as electronic journal articles.
- It replaces the URL in the reference.
- It is a permanent link to the online location of the article, so no access date is needed.
- Include: Available at: doi: xxxxxx at the end of the reference.

EXAMPLE:

> Available at: http://doi.org/52.169/deafed/tjd171.

Formatting Reference List

Below, the different types of the materials you may use in your work both in text and in reference list are shown with examples.

The section is divided into the following groups of sources:

BOOKS

Book (One Author)

GENERAL FORMAT:

    Surname, INITIALS. (year) *Title*. Place of publication: Name of publisher.

EXAMPLE:

    Smith, E. (2012) *Key issues in education and social justice*. London: SAGE.

IN-TEXT CITATION EXAMPLE:

    It has been argued that… (Smith, 2012:15).

Book (Several Authors)

GENERAL FORMAT:

    Surname, INITIALS., Surname, INITIALS. & Surname, INITIALS. (year) *Title*. Place of publication: Name of publisher.

EXAMPLE:

    Fumoto, H., Greenfield, S., Hargreaves, D. J. & Robson, S. (2012) *Young children's creative thinking*. London: SAGE.

IN-TEXT CITATION EXAMPLE:

    Fumoto et al. (2012:25) assert that 'there is an inherent difficulty in trying to define creativity'.

Chapter in an Edited Book

GENERAL FORMAT:

Surname of chapter author, INITIALS. (year) 'Chapter title'. In surname of editor, INITIALS. (ed) *Title of book*. Place of publication: Name of publisher. chapter pages.

EXAMPLE:

Eady, S. (2012) 'Personal professional development'. In Hansen, A. (ed.) *Primary professional studies*. 2nd edn. London: Learning Matters. pp.172-188.

IN-TEXT CITATION EXAMPLE:

Eady (2012:172) provides a helpful description of personal professional development...

E-Book

GENERAL FORMAT:

Surname, INITIALS. (year) *Title*. Place of publication: Name of publisher. Available at: URL or DOI*[Accessed: date].

EXAMPLE:

Hutchin, V. (2013) *Effective practice in the early years foundation stage: an essential guide*. Maidenhead: Oxford University Press. Available at: http://ebookcentral.proquest.com/lib/herts/reader.action?docID=1170014 [Accessed:28.12.19].

IN-TEXT CITATION EXAMPLE:

Children's confidence can be developed through play (Hutchin, 2013).

E-Book on E-Reader (Kindle Version)

GENERAL FORMAT:

Surname, INITIALS. (year) *Title*. Place of publication: publisher name [make & model of device].Available at: URL [Downloaded: date].

EXAMPLE:

>Peacock, A. (2016) *Assessment for learning without limits*. London: McGraw-Hill [Kindle edition]. Available at: https://goo.gl/3qzK2Q [Downloaded: 29.12.19]

IN-TEXT CITATION EXAMPLE:

>Peacock (2016:loc. 170) states that, 'pedagogy, curriculum and assessment are the core areas of expertise that form the foundations for all good teaching'.

Encyclopaedia

GENERAL FORMAT:

>Section author's surname(s), INITIALS. (year) 'Title of section'. In Editor(s) surname(s), INTITALS. *Title of Encyclopaedia*. Edition. Volume. Page numbers. Place of publication: Name of publisher.

EXAMPLE:

>Lowe, P.A. (2014) 'Attention-deficit/hyperactivity disorder'. In Reynolds, C.R., Vannest, K.J. & Fletcher-Janzen, E. *Encyclopedia of special education*. 4th edn. Vol. 1. pp. 251-256. Hoboken, NJ: John Wiley.

IN-TEXT CITATION EXAMPLE:

>According to Lowe (2014:251) 'Attention-Deficit/Hyperactivity Disorder (ADHD) is one of the most common disorders found among children'.

Dictionary

GENERAL FORMAT:

>Surname(s), INITIALS. (ed) (year) *Title*. (Edition) Place of publication: Name of publisher.

EXAMPLE:

>Soanes, C. (ed) (2006) *Concise Oxford English dictionary*. (11th edn. rev.) Oxford: Oxford University Press.

IN-TEXT CITATION EXAMPLE:

Pedagogy is defined as 'the profession, science, or theory of teaching' (Soanes, 2006:1055).

ARTICLES

Journal Article (One Author)

GENERAL FORMAT:

Surname, INITIALS. (year) 'Article Title'. *Journal title.* Volume number(issue number) pages.

EXAMPLE:

Lomas, T. (2017) 'Coherence in primary history'. *Primary History.* 76 summer. pp. 8-12.

IN-TEXT CITATION EXAMPLE:

Lomas (2017) believes that there is a variation in coherence according to both age and pupil development.

Journal Article (Several Authors)

GENERAL FORMAT:

Surname, INITIALS., Surname, INITIALS. & Surname, INITIALS (year) 'Article Title'. *Journal title.* Volume number(issue number) pages.

EXAMPLE:

Archer, L., DeWitt, J., & Wong, B. (2014) 'Spheres of influence: what shapes young people's aspirations at age 12/13 and what are the implications for education policy?' *Journal of Education Policy.* 29(1) pp.58-85. Available at: http://dx.doi.org/10.1080/02680939.2013.790079 .

IN-TEXT CITATION EXAMPLE:

Archer et al. (2014:77) argue that, 'aspirations form part of the ongoing social reproduction of privilege /disadvantage – despite being held up by education policy as a tool for social mobility and change'.

Online Journal Article

GENERAL FORMAT:

> Surname, INITIALS. (year) 'Article Title'. *Journal title.* Volume number(issue number) pages. Available at: URL or DOI [Accessed: date].

EXAMPLE:

> Dweck, C. (2015) Growth. *British Journal of Educational Psychology.* 85(2) pp. 242-245. Available at: http://doi.org/10.1111/bjep.12072 .

IN-TEXT CITATION EXAMPLE:

> "If… teachers believe that their own skills can be developed, each student provides an opportunity for them to learn more about their craft" (Dweck, 2015, p.244).

More than One Article (Same Author in the Same Year)

GENERAL FORMAT:

> Organization. (year a) 'Article Title'. *Journal title.* Volume number(issue number) pages.
>
> Organization. (year b) 'Article Title'. *Journal title.* Volume number(issue number) pages.

EXAMPLE:

> Wilkinson, A. (2017a) 'The gall nuts and lapis trail: what can you tell about Anglo-Saxon trade from ink?' *Primary History.* 76 summer. pp.28-30.
>
> Wilkinson, A. (2017b) 'Wot, no women? Did all Ancient Greek women stay at home and weave?' *Primary History.* 76 summer. pp.32-35.

IN-TEXT CITATION EXAMPLE:

> Wilkinson (2017a, 2017b) has written about these subjects in both Ancient and Anglo-Saxon history.

Newspaper, Magazine or Newsletter

GENERAL FORMAT:

Surname, INITIALS (year) 'Article title'. *Newspaper Title*. Date. Pages.

EXAMPLE:

Lee, J. (2016) 'Where are all the girls with autism?' *TES*. 22.4.16. pp. 29-34.

IN-TEXT CITATION EXAMPLE:

Lee (2016) suggests that indications of autism are often missed in girls.

OTHER ONLINE SOURCES

Website Page (With Author)

GENERAL FORMAT:

>Surname, INITIALS. (year) *Title*. Organization. Available at: URL [Accessed: date].

EXAMPLE:

>Izycky, A. (2010) *Does telling a story require both good language skills and 'theory of mind'?* BATOD. Available at: http://www.batod.org.uk/index.php?id=/resources/research/story-skill-tom.htm [Accessed: 28.12.19].

IN-TEXT CITATION EXAMPLE:

>Izycky (2010) conducted a literature review to explore findings regarding theory of mind in deaf children.

Website Page (Corporate Author)

GENERAL FORMAT:

>Corporate author / organization (year) *Title*. Available at: URL [Accessed: date].

EXAMPLE:

>BBC (2017) *SATs for seven-year-olds scrapped from 2023*. Available at: http://www.bbc.co.uk/news/education-41274741 [Accessed: 29.12.19].

IN-TEXT CITATION EXAMPLE:

>The BBC (2017) has reported on the government's announcement that SATs will not be compulsory from 2023.

Online Newspaper, Magazine or Newsletter

GENERAL FORMAT:

Surname, INITIALS (year) 'Article title'. *Newspaper Title*. Date. [online] Available at: URL [Accessed:date].

EXAMPLE:

Rosen, M. (2017) 'Dear Justine Greening: your primary school reading reforms aren't making the grade'. *The Guardian*. Available at: https://www.theguardian.com/education/2017/jul/25/reading-reforms-primary-schools-michael-rosen [Accessed: 28.12.19].

IN-TEXT CITATION EXAMPLE:

In July's 'Letter from a curious parent' author, Michael Rosen (2017) questions the beneficence of recent reading reforms and grammar tests.

SOCIAL MEDIA

You Tube Video

GENERAL FORMAT:

Surname of person posting video, INITIALS (Year posted) *Title of video*. Available at: URL [Accessed:date].

EXAMPLE:

Roberts, A. (2013) *Leadership is… distributed.* Available at: https://www.youtube.com/watch?v=J5F0MNrDSpY [Accessed 29.19.19].

Blogs / Vlogs

GENERAL FORMAT:

Surname, INITIAL. (year site published / updated) 'Title of message', *Title of internet site*, day & month of posted message. Available at: URL [Accessed: date].

EXAMPLE:

Walker, A. (2017) 'World Mental Health Day 2017: A Preventative Agenda for Mental Wellbeing', Huffington Post UK, 10 October. Available at: http://www.huffingtonpost.co.uk/angus-walker1/world-mental-health-day_b_18204824.html [Accessed: 28.12.19].

IN-TEXT CITATION EXAMPLE:

Walker (2017) discusses funding issues for mental health services.

Facebook

GENERAL FORMAT:

Surname, INITIAL. (year page published/updated) *Title of page* [Facebook] day & month of posted message. Available at: URL. [Accessed: date].

Twitter

GENERAL FORMAT:

Surname, INITIAL. (year tweet posted) [Twitter] day & month posted. Available at: URL [Accessed:date].

Instagram

GENERAL FORMAT:

Photographer Surname, INITIALS. (year) *Title of Photograph*. Available at: URL [Accessed: date].

LEGAL PUBLICATIONS

Legislation – UK Statutes (Acts of Parliament)

GENERAL FORMAT:

Title of Act including year and chapter number. Country if referencing more than one country's legislation). Available at: URL [Accessed: date].

EXAMPLE:

Education Act 2011 c.21. Available at: http://www.legislation.gov.uk/ukpga/2011/21/contents/enacted [Accessed: 29.12.19].

IN-TEXT CITATION EXAMPLE:

Section 76(1) of the Education Act (2011) states the requirement for student loans interest rates to be lower than the current market rate.

Government Publications

GENERAL FORMAT:

Government Department (year) *Title.* (Series if applicable). Place of publication: publisher. Available at: URL [Accessed: date].

EXAMPLE:

Department for Education (2017) *Statutory framework for the early years foundation stage: Setting the standards for learning, development and care for children from birth to five.* London: The Stationery Office. Available at: https://www.gov.uk/government/publications/early-years-foundation-stage-framework--2 [Accessed: 28.12.19].

IN-TEXT CITATION EXAMPLE:

According to the EYFS statutory framework (DfE, 2017) there are four overarching principles for practice.

Law Reports (Cases)

GENERAL FORMAT:
> '*Name of parties involved in case*' (year) *Court and case.* Court and case no. Available at: URL [Accessed: date].

EXAMPLE:
> 'Gillick v West Norfolk and Wisbech AHA' (1985) House of Lords UKHL 7. *BAILII.* Available at: http://www.bailii.org/uk/cases/UKHL/1985/7.html [Accessed: 29.12.19].

IN-TEXT CITATION EXAMPLE:
> Parliament clarified the provision of contraceptive advice for young people under the age of 16 (Gillick v West Norfolk and Wisbech AHA, 1985).

PART 4: FREQUENTLY ASKED QUESTIONS

1. **Are references included in my word count?**

Usually in-text citations will be included in your word count as they are integral to your argument. This may vary depending on the assignment you are writing and you should confirm this with your module tutor.

The reference list is not included in the word count of your paper.

2. **When must I use page numbers in my in-text citations?**

It is important to give a page number to an in-text citation in the following circumstances:
- *when quoting directly;*
- *when referring to a specific detail in a text (for example, a specific theory or idea, an illustration, a table, a set of statistics).*

Giving page numbers enables the reader to locate the specific item to which you refer.

3. **What if an author I am referencing has published two or more works in one year?**

In this case you can use lower-case letters: a, b, c, etc. to differentiate between different works within one given year.

In-text:

(Carroll, 2007a; Carroll 2007b)

Reference list:

Carroll, J. (2007a). A handbook for deterring plagiarism in higher education. Oxford: Oxford Centre for Staff and Learning Development, Oxford Brookes University.
Carroll, J. (2007b). Do national statistics about plagiarism tell you about your students? LINK Newsletter on Academic Integrity. The Hospitality, Sport and Leisure Subject Centre, 18, 3-9.

4. What is the difference between a reference list and a bibliography?

Most school assignments require a list of references at the end of your assignment and not a bibliography. They are similar in that they both use the Harvard system and have full references, listed in alphabetical order of the author(s) surname(s).

References are the items you have read and specifically referred to (or cited) in your assignment. You are expected to list these references at the end of your assignment in a reference list. A reference list will include all the references that you have cited in the text.

A bibliography is sometimes used to refer to a list of everything you consulted in preparation for writing your assignment or used as background reading for your assignment, whether or not you referred specifically to or cited in the assignment. Do not make a long Bibliography to impress; only include items that you think provide useful information for the reader.

You would normally only have one list, headed 'references' or 'bibliography', and you should check with your department which you are required to provide.

PART 5: PAPER LAYOUT EXAMPLE

The Harvard Essay Template   1

THE HARVARD ESSAY TEMPLATE

by (Name)

The Name of the Class (Course)

Professor (Tutor)

The Name of the School (University)

The City and State where it is located

The Date

The Harvard Essay Template: The Essay Title is Centered and Capitalized

The first paragraph of the essay introduces the reader to your topic with a "hook," which might be an interesting fact, a statistic, or a lively quotation that sheds light on your essay.

Centered Headings to Break Up the Body of the Essay

Italicized Headings for Subsections

The first sentence of the first body paragraph should be the topic sentence, which tells the reader what the paragraph will discuss. After the topic sentence, supporting details are used to provide more information about it. Details can include analysis, explanation, quotations about the subject, and/or facts and figures that support the topic sentence. The paragraph should conclude with a sentence that sums up the paragraph and leads into the next body paragraph.

New Subheadings to Introduce New Subtopics

You should show how your next paragraph connects to the one that came before. The paragraph should have its own topic sentence and follow the same body paragraph, with supporting details and a closing sentence.

New Heading When You Change Major Topics

Within your paragraphs, you should be sure to cite your sources using in-text citations. Harvard style typically asks students to use a standard font (such as Times New Roman, Arial, etc.) at size 12 pt. You should not use fancy fonts, colors in the text, or excessive amounts of boldface, underlining, or italics.

The Conclusion of the Essay

The first sentence of the conclusion should remind the reader in different words what the essay has shown. You should then offer a brief discussion of your topic to remind the reader what the most important parts of the essay were. You should finish your essay with the single most important point you want the reader to remember. Following the conclusion is the reference list, which lists on a separate page all the sources used in the in-text citations, and only the sources used in-text.

References

Adams, J. Hayes, J. & Hopson, B. (1976) *Understanding and managing personal change.* London: Martin Robertson. Cited in Bassot, B. (2013) *The Reflective Journal.* Basingstoke: Palgrave Macmillan. pp 4-5.

Archer, L., DeWitt, J., & Wong, B. (2014) Spheres of influence: what shapes young people's aspirations at age 12/13 and what are the implications for education policy? *Journal of Education Policy.* 29(1) pp.58-85. Available at: http://dx.doi.org/10.1080/02680939.2013.790079.

BBC (2017) *SATs for seven-year-olds scrapped from 2023.* Available at: http://www.bbc.co.uk/news/education-41274741 [Accessed: 19.12.19].

Beck, U. (1992) *Risk Society.* London: Sage. Cited in Holdsworth, C. (2010) 'Why volunteer? Understanding motivations for student volunteering'. *British Journal of Educational Studies.* 58(4). 421-437. Available at: http://dx.doi.org/10.1080/00071005.2010.527666.

Bruner, J. S. 1974. *Toward a theory of instruction.* Cambridge, MA: Harvard University Press.

Dweck, C. (2015) Growth. *British Journal of Educational Psychology.* 85(2) pp. 242-245. Available at: http://dx.doi.org/10.1111/bjep.12072.

Eady, S. (2012) 'Personal professional development'. In Hansen, A. (ed.) *Primary professional studies.* 2nd edn. London: Learning Matters. pp.172-188.

Education Act 2011 c.21. Available at: http://www.legislation.gov.uk/ukpga/2011/21/

contents/enacted [Accessed: 12.12.19].

Fumoto, H., Greenfield, S., Hargreaves, D. J. & Robson, S. (2012) *Young children's creative thinking.* London: SAGE.

'Gillick v West Norfolk and Wisbech AHA' (1985) House of Lords UKHL 7. *BAILII* Available at: http://www.bailii.org/uk/cases/UKHL/1985/7.html [Accessed: 20.12.19].

Grant, S. (2017) *Structure and Assessment Regulations - Undergraduate and Taught Postgraduate Programmes (UPR AS14) Appendix III, Assessment Offences, version 10.0.* Available at: http://sitem.herts.ac.uk/secreg/upr/pdf/AS14-Apx3-Assessment%20Offences-v10.0.pdf [Accessed: 21.12.19].

Hutchin, V. (2013) *Effective Practice in the Early years foundation stage: an essential guide.* Maidenhead: Oxford University Press. Available at: http://ebookcentral.proquest.com/lib/herts/reader.action?docID=1170014 [Accessed: 12.12.19].

Kyriacou, C., & Kunc, R. (2007). Beginning teachers' expectations of teaching. *Teaching and Teacher Education.* 23(8) pp. 1246-1257. Available at: https://doi.org/10.1016/j.tate.2006.06.002 .

Lee, J. (2016) 'Where are all the girls with autism?' *TES.* 22.4.16. pp. 29-34.

Lomas, T. (2017) 'Coherence in primary History'. *Primary History.* 76 summer. pp. 8-12.

Lowe, P.A. & Reynolds, C.R. (2014) 'Attention-deficit/hyperactivity disorder'. In Reynolds, C.R., Vannest, K.J. & Fletcher-Janzen, E. *Encyclopedia of special education.* 4th edn. Vol. 1. pp. 251-256. Hoboken, NJ: John Wiley.

Matisse in the Studio (2017) [Exhibition] Royal Academy of Arts, London. 5 August 2017 – 12 November 2017.

Neshat, S. (2005) *Hands*. [photograph]. Available at: http://www.artnet.com/artists/shirin-neshat/hands-a-5KqX4k-pTtqIEAs31T3L9A2 [Accessed: 23.12.19]

Ordnance Survey (2015) *St Albans & Hatfield*. Sheet 182, 1:25,000. Southampton: Ordnance Survey (OS Explorer series).

Peacock, A. (2016) *Assessment for learning without limits*. London: McGraw-Hill [Kindle edition]. Available at: https://goo.gl/3qzK2Q [Downloaded: 31.10.17].

Pears, R. & Shields, G. (2016) *Cite them right: the essential referencing guide*. 10th edn. London: Palgrave.

Robertson, J. 1986. The economics of local recovery. In: *The other economic summit, 17/18 April 1986, Tokyo*. London: The Other Economic Summit. pp. 5-10.

Rogers, B. (1997) *You know the fair rule*. 2nd edn. London: Pitman.

Soanes, C. & Stevenson, A. (eds) (2006) *Concise Oxford English dictionary* (11th edn. rev.) Oxford: Oxford University Press.

University of Hertfordshire (2017a) *About Us*. Available at: http://www.herts.ac.uk/about-us [Accessed: 19.12.19].

University of Hertfordshire (2017b) *About the School of Education*. Available at: http://www.herts.ac.uk/apply/schools-of-study/education/about-us [Accessed: 19.12.19].

University of Hertfordshire (2017c) *MA Education Framework*. Available at: http://www.herts.ac.uk/apply/schools-of-study/education/postgraduate-courses/ma-education-framework [Accessed: 19.12.19].

van Gogh, V. (1888) *Sunflowers* [oil on canvas]. The National Gallery, London.

Wilkinson, A. (2017a) 'The gall nuts and lapis trail: what can you tell about Anglo-Saxon trade from ink?' *Primary History*. 76

summer. pp. 28-30.

Wilkinson, A. (2017b) 'Wot, no women? Did all Ancient Greek women stay at home and weave?' *Primary History.* 76 summer. pp. 32-35.

Note: *For the purpose of demonstrating a variety of references, this page contains references that do not match the preceding paper. This is only a sample of how a reference list might be laid out at the end of your essay.*

Please remember: *In a real paper, only the sources you have actually read are referenced in the bibliography/reference list.*

SOURCES

Harvard format is only one of many methods of documentation.

There are several variations of Harvard style used in different countries; this guide is the most common format but is not the only one in use.

Further information may be found in your school's Harvard style guide.

The instructor for your class is the final authority on how to format your References List.

Students may also wish to check the following website for information on Harvard format:
- http://owl.english.purdue.edu

Reference management software

There are several free useful reference management software apps (e.g. EndNote) to help you manage your references.

Printed in Great Britain
by Amazon